This journal belongs to:

_____

_____

_____

"Many eyes go through the meadow,
but few see the flowers in it"
   - Ralph Waldo Emerson

Daily Journal

THINGS WE ARE GRATEFUL FOR EACH DAY CAN SOMETIMES BE BIG THINGS, BUT MORE OFTEN THAN NOT THEY ARE LITTLE THINGS THAT MIGHT GO UNNOTICED IF WE DON'T STOP TO THINK ABOUT WHAT THEY ARE. IT COULD BE THAT THE SUN WAS SHINING, OR A SONG YOU LOVE CAME ON THE RADIO AT JUST THE RIGHT TIME. IT CAN ALSO BE AS SIMPLE AS A CUP OF HOT APPLE CIDER ON A COLD FALL DAY OR FOR THE WAY SOMETHING SMELLS THAT REMINDS US OF A SPECIAL MEMORY.

WRITING THESE THINGS DOWN EACH DAY CAN HELP US FEEL BETTER ABOUT THE DAY, EVEN ON THE BAD DAYS. AS YOU COMPLETE THIS JOURNAL, YOU'LL START TO HAVE A COLLECTION OF THE LITTLE THINGS THAT BRING YOU HAPPINESS.

STARTING A HABIT TO KEEP TRACK OF WHAT YOU ARE GRATEFUL FOR DOESN'T MEAN OF COURSE, THAT THERE WON'T ALSO BE DIFFICULT

PARTS TO MANY DAYS. SOME MORE THAN
OTHERS. KEEP TRACK OF YOUR DAILY WINS,
AND ALSO CHALLENGES YOU HAVE FACED AND
WORKED THROUGH - THAT WAY WHEN LIFE DOES
BRING SOMETHING MORE DIFFICULT, YOU'LL HAVE
CONFIDENCE IN YOUR ABILITY TO HANDLE IT -
EVEN WHEN THINGS DO NOT GO PERFECT OR EASY.

THE DAILY DOODLE IS A PLACE TO BE CREATIVE,
RELAX AND GET OUT OF YOUR HEAD.

GIVE YOURSELF A FEW MINUTES EACH DAY
TO WRITE YOUR THOUGHTS AND TO CAPTURE
MOMENTS YOU'LL WANT TO LOOK BACK ON AND
REMEMBER.

THIS JOURNAL CAN BE A GREAT ADDITION TO
YOUR MORNING OR NIGHTTIME ROUTINE. USE IT
TO TRACK PROGRESS, SEE PATTERNS AND LEARN
MORE ABOUT WHAT IS MOST IMPORTANT TO YOU.
YOU'LL THANK YOURSELF FOR IT LATER!

Daily Gratitudes

DATE: _____

THREE (LITTLE OR BIG) THINGS THAT WERE GOOD TODAY:

1. _____

2. _____

3. _____

THE BEST THING IN MY DAY TODAY:

_____

_____

SOMETHING DIFFICULT I WAS ABLE TO WORK THROUGH:

_____

_____

DAILY DOODLE:

DATE: _____

THREE (LITTLE OR BIG) THINGS THAT WERE GOOD TODAY:

1. _____

2. _____

3. _____

THE BEST THING IN MY DAY TODAY:

_____

_____

SOMETHING DIFFICULT I WAS ABLE TO WORK THROUGH:

_____

_____

DAILY DOODLE:

DATE: _____

THREE (LITTLE OR BIG) THINGS THAT WERE GOOD TODAY:

1. _____

2. _____

3. _____

THE BEST THING IN MY DAY TODAY:

_____

_____

SOMETHING DIFFICULT I WAS ABLE TO WORK THROUGH:

_____

_____

DAILY DOODLE:

DATE: _____

THREE (LITTLE OR BIG) THINGS THAT WERE GOOD TODAY:

1. _____

2. _____

3. _____

THE BEST THING IN MY DAY TODAY:

_____

_____

SOMETHING DIFFICULT I WAS ABLE TO WORK THROUGH:

_____

_____

DAILY DOODLE:

DATE: _____

THREE (LITTLE OR BIG) THINGS THAT WERE GOOD TODAY:

1. _____

2. _____

3. _____

THE BEST THING IN MY DAY TODAY:

_____

_____

SOMETHING DIFFICULT I WAS ABLE TO WORK THROUGH:

_____

_____

DAILY DOODLE:

DATE: _____

THREE (LITTLE OR BIG) THINGS THAT WERE GOOD TODAY:

1. _____

2. _____

3. _____

THE BEST THING IN MY DAY TODAY:

_____

_____

SOMETHING DIFFICULT I WAS ABLE TO WORK THROUGH:

_____

_____

DAILY DOODLE:

DATE: _____

THREE (LITTLE OR BIG) THINGS THAT WERE GOOD TODAY:
1. _____
2. _____
3. _____

THE BEST THING IN MY DAY TODAY:
_____
_____

SOMETHING DIFFICULT I WAS ABLE TO WORK THROUGH:
_____
_____

DAILY DOODLE:

DATE: _____

THREE (LITTLE OR BIG) THINGS THAT WERE GOOD TODAY:
1. _____
2. _____
3. _____

THE BEST THING IN MY DAY TODAY:
_____
_____

SOMETHING DIFFICULT I WAS ABLE TO WORK THROUGH:
_____
_____

DAILY DOODLE:

DATE: _____

THREE (LITTLE OR BIG) THINGS THAT WERE GOOD TODAY:

1. _____

2. _____

3. _____

THE BEST THING IN MY DAY TODAY:

_____

_____

SOMETHING DIFFICULT I WAS ABLE TO WORK THROUGH:

_____

_____

DAILY DOODLE:

DATE: _____

THREE (LITTLE OR BIG) THINGS THAT WERE GOOD TODAY:

1. _____

2. _____

3. _____

THE BEST THING IN MY DAY TODAY:

_____

_____

SOMETHING DIFFICULT I WAS ABLE TO WORK THROUGH:

_____

_____

DAILY DOODLE:

DATE: _____

THREE (LITTLE OR BIG) THINGS THAT WERE GOOD TODAY:

1. _____

2. _____

3. _____

THE BEST THING IN MY DAY TODAY:

_____

_____

SOMETHING DIFFICULT I WAS ABLE TO WORK THROUGH:

_____

_____

DAILY DOODLE:

DATE: _____

THREE (LITTLE OR BIG) THINGS THAT WERE GOOD TODAY:

1. _____

2. _____

3. _____

THE BEST THING IN MY DAY TODAY:

_____

_____

SOMETHING DIFFICULT I WAS ABLE TO WORK THROUGH:

_____

_____

DAILY DOODLE:

DATE: _____

THREE (LITTLE OR BIG) THINGS THAT WERE GOOD TODAY:

1. _____

2. _____

3. _____

THE BEST THING IN MY DAY TODAY:

_____

_____

SOMETHING DIFFICULT I WAS ABLE TO WORK THROUGH:

_____

_____

DAILY DOODLE:

DATE: _____

THREE (LITTLE OR BIG) THINGS THAT WERE GOOD TODAY:

1. _____

2. _____

3. _____

THE BEST THING IN MY DAY TODAY:

_____

_____

SOMETHING DIFFICULT I WAS ABLE TO WORK THROUGH:

_____

_____

DAILY DOODLE:

DATE: _____

THREE (LITTLE OR BIG) THINGS THAT WERE GOOD TODAY:

1. _____

2. _____

3. _____

THE BEST THING IN MY DAY TODAY:

_____

_____

SOMETHING DIFFICULT I WAS ABLE TO WORK THROUGH:

_____

_____

DAILY DOODLE:

DATE: _____

THREE (LITTLE OR BIG) THINGS THAT WERE GOOD TODAY:

1. _____

2. _____

3. _____

THE BEST THING IN MY DAY TODAY:

_____

_____

SOMETHING DIFFICULT I WAS ABLE TO WORK THROUGH:

_____

_____

DAILY DOODLE:

DATE: _____

THREE (LITTLE OR BIG) THINGS THAT WERE GOOD TODAY:

1. _____

2. _____

3. _____

THE BEST THING IN MY DAY TODAY:

_____

_____

SOMETHING DIFFICULT I WAS ABLE TO WORK THROUGH:

_____

_____

DAILY DOODLE:

DATE: _____

THREE (LITTLE OR BIG) THINGS THAT WERE GOOD TODAY:

1. _____

2. _____

3. _____

THE BEST THING IN MY DAY TODAY:

_____

_____

SOMETHING DIFFICULT I WAS ABLE TO WORK THROUGH:

_____

_____

DAILY DOODLE:

DATE: _____

THREE (LITTLE OR BIG) THINGS THAT WERE GOOD TODAY:

1. _____

2. _____

3. _____

THE BEST THING IN MY DAY TODAY:

_____

_____

SOMETHING DIFFICULT I WAS ABLE TO WORK THROUGH:

_____

_____

DAILY DOODLE:

DATE: _____

THREE (LITTLE OR BIG) THINGS THAT WERE GOOD TODAY:

1. _____

2. _____

3. _____

THE BEST THING IN MY DAY TODAY:

_____

_____

SOMETHING DIFFICULT I WAS ABLE TO WORK THROUGH:

_____

_____

DAILY DOODLE:

DATE: _____

THREE (LITTLE OR BIG) THINGS THAT WERE GOOD TODAY:

1. _____
2. _____
3. _____

THE BEST THING IN MY DAY TODAY:

_____
_____

SOMETHING DIFFICULT I WAS ABLE TO WORK THROUGH:

_____
_____

DAILY DOODLE:

DATE: _____

THREE (LITTLE OR BIG) THINGS THAT WERE GOOD TODAY:

1. _____
2. _____
3. _____

THE BEST THING IN MY DAY TODAY:

_____
_____

SOMETHING DIFFICULT I WAS ABLE TO WORK THROUGH:

_____
_____

DAILY DOODLE:

DATE:

THREE (LITTLE OR BIG) THINGS THAT WERE GOOD TODAY:
1.
2.
3.

THE BEST THING IN MY DAY TODAY:

SOMETHING DIFFICULT I WAS ABLE TO WORK THROUGH:

DAILY DOODLE:

DATE:

THREE (LITTLE OR BIG) THINGS THAT WERE GOOD TODAY:
1.
2.
3.

THE BEST THING IN MY DAY TODAY:

SOMETHING DIFFICULT I WAS ABLE TO WORK THROUGH:

DAILY DOODLE:

DATE: _____

THREE (LITTLE OR BIG) THINGS THAT WERE GOOD TODAY:

1. _____

2. _____

3. _____

THE BEST THING IN MY DAY TODAY:

_____

_____

SOMETHING DIFFICULT I WAS ABLE TO WORK THROUGH:

_____

_____

DAILY DOODLE:

DATE: _____

THREE (LITTLE OR BIG) THINGS THAT WERE GOOD TODAY:

1. _____

2. _____

3. _____

THE BEST THING IN MY DAY TODAY:

_____

_____

SOMETHING DIFFICULT I WAS ABLE TO WORK THROUGH:

_____

_____

DAILY DOODLE:

DATE: _____

THREE (LITTLE OR BIG) THINGS THAT WERE GOOD TODAY:

1. _____

2. _____

3. _____

THE BEST THING IN MY DAY TODAY:

_____

_____

SOMETHING DIFFICULT I WAS ABLE TO WORK THROUGH:

_____

_____

DAILY DOODLE:

DATE: _____

THREE (LITTLE OR BIG) THINGS THAT WERE GOOD TODAY:

1. _____

2. _____

3. _____

THE BEST THING IN MY DAY TODAY:

_____

_____

SOMETHING DIFFICULT I WAS ABLE TO WORK THROUGH:

_____

_____

DAILY DOODLE:

DATE: _____

THREE (LITTLE OR BIG) THINGS THAT WERE GOOD TODAY:

1. _____

2. _____

3. _____

THE BEST THING IN MY DAY TODAY:

_____

_____

SOMETHING DIFFICULT I WAS ABLE TO WORK THROUGH:

_____

_____

DAILY DOODLE:

DATE: _____

THREE (LITTLE OR BIG) THINGS THAT WERE GOOD TODAY:

1. _____

2. _____

3. _____

THE BEST THING IN MY DAY TODAY:

_____

_____

SOMETHING DIFFICULT I WAS ABLE TO WORK THROUGH:

_____

_____

DAILY DOODLE:

DATE: _____

THREE (LITTLE OR BIG) THINGS THAT WERE GOOD TODAY:

1. _____

2. _____

3. _____

THE BEST THING IN MY DAY TODAY:

_____

_____

SOMETHING DIFFICULT I WAS ABLE TO WORK THROUGH:

_____

_____

DAILY DOODLE:

DATE: _____

THREE (LITTLE OR BIG) THINGS THAT WERE GOOD TODAY:

1. _____

2. _____

3. _____

THE BEST THING IN MY DAY TODAY:

_____

_____

SOMETHING DIFFICULT I WAS ABLE TO WORK THROUGH:

_____

_____

DAILY DOODLE:

DATE:

THREE (LITTLE OR BIG) THINGS THAT WERE GOOD TODAY:

1.

2.

3.

THE BEST THING IN MY DAY TODAY:

SOMETHING DIFFICULT I WAS ABLE TO WORK THROUGH:

DAILY DOODLE:

DATE:

THREE (LITTLE OR BIG) THINGS THAT WERE GOOD TODAY:

1.

2.

3.

THE BEST THING IN MY DAY TODAY:

SOMETHING DIFFICULT I WAS ABLE TO WORK THROUGH:

DAILY DOODLE:

DATE: _____

THREE (LITTLE OR BIG) THINGS THAT WERE GOOD TODAY:

1. _____

2. _____

3. _____

THE BEST THING IN MY DAY TODAY:

_____

_____

SOMETHING DIFFICULT I WAS ABLE TO WORK THROUGH:

_____

_____

DAILY DOODLE:

DATE: _____

THREE (LITTLE OR BIG) THINGS THAT WERE GOOD TODAY:

1. _____

2. _____

3. _____

THE BEST THING IN MY DAY TODAY:

_____

_____

SOMETHING DIFFICULT I WAS ABLE TO WORK THROUGH:

_____

_____

DAILY DOODLE:

DATE:

THREE (LITTLE OR BIG) THINGS THAT WERE GOOD TODAY:

1.

2.

3.

THE BEST THING IN MY DAY TODAY:

SOMETHING DIFFICULT I WAS ABLE TO WORK THROUGH:

DAILY DOODLE:

DATE:

THREE (LITTLE OR BIG) THINGS THAT WERE GOOD TODAY:

1.

2.

3.

THE BEST THING IN MY DAY TODAY:

SOMETHING DIFFICULT I WAS ABLE TO WORK THROUGH:

DAILY DOODLE:

DATE: _____

THREE (LITTLE OR BIG) THINGS THAT WERE GOOD TODAY:
1. _____
2. _____
3. _____

THE BEST THING IN MY DAY TODAY:
_____
_____

SOMETHING DIFFICULT I WAS ABLE TO WORK THROUGH:
_____
_____

DAILY DOODLE:

DATE: _____

THREE (LITTLE OR BIG) THINGS THAT WERE GOOD TODAY:
1. _____
2. _____
3. _____

THE BEST THING IN MY DAY TODAY:
_____
_____

SOMETHING DIFFICULT I WAS ABLE TO WORK THROUGH:
_____
_____

DAILY DOODLE:

DATE: _____

THREE (LITTLE OR BIG) THINGS THAT WERE GOOD TODAY:

1. _____

2. _____

3. _____

THE BEST THING IN MY DAY TODAY:

_____

_____

SOMETHING DIFFICULT I WAS ABLE TO WORK THROUGH:

_____

_____

DAILY DOODLE:

DATE: _____

THREE (LITTLE OR BIG) THINGS THAT WERE GOOD TODAY:

1. _____

2. _____

3. _____

THE BEST THING IN MY DAY TODAY:

_____

_____

SOMETHING DIFFICULT I WAS ABLE TO WORK THROUGH:

_____

_____

DAILY DOODLE:

DATE: _____

THREE (LITTLE OR BIG) THINGS THAT WERE GOOD TODAY:

1. _____

2. _____

3. _____

THE BEST THING IN MY DAY TODAY:

_____

_____

SOMETHING DIFFICULT I WAS ABLE TO WORK THROUGH:

_____

_____

DAILY DOODLE:

DATE: _____

THREE (LITTLE OR BIG) THINGS THAT WERE GOOD TODAY:

1. _____

2. _____

3. _____

THE BEST THING IN MY DAY TODAY:

_____

_____

SOMETHING DIFFICULT I WAS ABLE TO WORK THROUGH:

_____

_____

DAILY DOODLE:

DATE:

THREE (LITTLE OR BIG) THINGS THAT WERE GOOD TODAY:

1.

2.

3.

THE BEST THING IN MY DAY TODAY:

SOMETHING DIFFICULT I WAS ABLE TO WORK THROUGH:

DAILY DOODLE:

DATE:

THREE (LITTLE OR BIG) THINGS THAT WERE GOOD TODAY:

1.

2.

3.

THE BEST THING IN MY DAY TODAY:

SOMETHING DIFFICULT I WAS ABLE TO WORK THROUGH:

DAILY DOODLE:

DATE: _____

THREE (LITTLE OR BIG) THINGS THAT WERE GOOD TODAY:

1. _____

2. _____

3. _____

THE BEST THING IN MY DAY TODAY:

_____

_____

SOMETHING DIFFICULT I WAS ABLE TO WORK THROUGH:

_____

_____

DAILY DOODLE:

DATE: _____

THREE (LITTLE OR BIG) THINGS THAT WERE GOOD TODAY:

1. _____

2. _____

3. _____

THE BEST THING IN MY DAY TODAY:

_____

_____

SOMETHING DIFFICULT I WAS ABLE TO WORK THROUGH:

_____

_____

DAILY DOODLE:

DATE: _____

THREE (LITTLE OR BIG) THINGS THAT WERE GOOD TODAY:
1. _____
2. _____
3. _____

THE BEST THING IN MY DAY TODAY:
_____
_____

SOMETHING DIFFICULT I WAS ABLE TO WORK THROUGH:
_____
_____

DAILY DOODLE:

DATE: _____

THREE (LITTLE OR BIG) THINGS THAT WERE GOOD TODAY:
1. _____
2. _____
3. _____

THE BEST THING IN MY DAY TODAY:
_____
_____

SOMETHING DIFFICULT I WAS ABLE TO WORK THROUGH:
_____
_____

DAILY DOODLE:

DATE: _____

THREE (LITTLE OR BIG) THINGS THAT WERE GOOD TODAY:

1. _____

2. _____

3. _____

THE BEST THING IN MY DAY TODAY:

_____

_____

SOMETHING DIFFICULT I WAS ABLE TO WORK THROUGH:

_____

_____

DAILY DOODLE:

DATE: _____

THREE (LITTLE OR BIG) THINGS THAT WERE GOOD TODAY:

1. _____

2. _____

3. _____

THE BEST THING IN MY DAY TODAY:

_____

_____

SOMETHING DIFFICULT I WAS ABLE TO WORK THROUGH:

_____

_____

DAILY DOODLE:

DATE: _____

THREE (LITTLE OR BIG) THINGS THAT WERE GOOD TODAY:

1. _____

2. _____

3. _____

THE BEST THING IN MY DAY TODAY:

_____

_____

SOMETHING DIFFICULT I WAS ABLE TO WORK THROUGH:

_____

_____

DAILY DOODLE:

DATE: _____

THREE (LITTLE OR BIG) THINGS THAT WERE GOOD TODAY:

1. _____

2. _____

3. _____

THE BEST THING IN MY DAY TODAY:

_____

_____

SOMETHING DIFFICULT I WAS ABLE TO WORK THROUGH:

_____

_____

DAILY DOODLE:

DATE: _____

THREE (LITTLE OR BIG) THINGS THAT WERE GOOD TODAY:

1. _____

2. _____

3. _____

THE BEST THING IN MY DAY TODAY:

_____

_____

SOMETHING DIFFICULT I WAS ABLE TO WORK THROUGH:

_____

_____

DAILY DOODLE:

DATE: _____

THREE (LITTLE OR BIG) THINGS THAT WERE GOOD TODAY:

1. _____

2. _____

3. _____

THE BEST THING IN MY DAY TODAY:

_____

_____

SOMETHING DIFFICULT I WAS ABLE TO WORK THROUGH:

_____

_____

DAILY DOODLE:

DATE: _____

THREE (LITTLE OR BIG) THINGS THAT WERE GOOD TODAY:

1. _____

2. _____

3. _____

THE BEST THING IN MY DAY TODAY:

_____

_____

SOMETHING DIFFICULT I WAS ABLE TO WORK THROUGH:

_____

_____

DAILY DOODLE:

DATE: _____

THREE (LITTLE OR BIG) THINGS THAT WERE GOOD TODAY:

1. _____

2. _____

3. _____

THE BEST THING IN MY DAY TODAY:

_____

_____

SOMETHING DIFFICULT I WAS ABLE TO WORK THROUGH:

_____

_____

DAILY DOODLE:

DATE: _____

THREE (LITTLE OR BIG) THINGS THAT WERE GOOD TODAY:

1. _____

2. _____

3. _____

THE BEST THING IN MY DAY TODAY:

_____

_____

SOMETHING DIFFICULT I WAS ABLE TO WORK THROUGH:

_____

_____

DAILY DOODLE:

DATE: _____

THREE (LITTLE OR BIG) THINGS THAT WERE GOOD TODAY:

1. _____

2. _____

3. _____

THE BEST THING IN MY DAY TODAY:

_____

_____

SOMETHING DIFFICULT I WAS ABLE TO WORK THROUGH:

_____

_____

DAILY DOODLE:

DATE: _____

THREE (LITTLE OR BIG) THINGS THAT WERE GOOD TODAY:

1. _____

2. _____

3. _____

THE BEST THING IN MY DAY TODAY:

_____

_____

SOMETHING DIFFICULT I WAS ABLE TO WORK THROUGH:

_____

_____

DAILY DOODLE:

DATE: _____

THREE (LITTLE OR BIG) THINGS THAT WERE GOOD TODAY:

1. _____

2. _____

3. _____

THE BEST THING IN MY DAY TODAY:

_____

_____

SOMETHING DIFFICULT I WAS ABLE TO WORK THROUGH:

_____

_____

DAILY DOODLE:

DATE: _____

THREE (LITTLE OR BIG) THINGS THAT WERE GOOD TODAY:

1. _____

2. _____

3. _____

THE BEST THING IN MY DAY TODAY:

_____

_____

SOMETHING DIFFICULT I WAS ABLE TO WORK THROUGH:

_____

_____

DAILY DOODLE:

DATE: _____

THREE (LITTLE OR BIG) THINGS THAT WERE GOOD TODAY:

1. _____

2. _____

3. _____

THE BEST THING IN MY DAY TODAY:

_____

_____

SOMETHING DIFFICULT I WAS ABLE TO WORK THROUGH:

_____

_____

DAILY DOODLE:

DATE: _____

THREE (LITTLE OR BIG) THINGS THAT WERE GOOD TODAY:

1. _____

2. _____

3. _____

THE BEST THING IN MY DAY TODAY:

_____

_____

SOMETHING DIFFICULT I WAS ABLE TO WORK THROUGH:

_____

_____

DAILY DOODLE:

DATE: _____

THREE (LITTLE OR BIG) THINGS THAT WERE GOOD TODAY:

1. _____

2. _____

3. _____

THE BEST THING IN MY DAY TODAY:

_____

_____

SOMETHING DIFFICULT I WAS ABLE TO WORK THROUGH:

_____

_____

DAILY DOODLE:

DATE: _____

THREE (LITTLE OR BIG) THINGS THAT WERE GOOD TODAY:

1. _____

2. _____

3. _____

THE BEST THING IN MY DAY TODAY:

_____

_____

SOMETHING DIFFICULT I WAS ABLE TO WORK THROUGH:

_____

_____

DAILY DOODLE:

DATE: _____

THREE (LITTLE OR BIG) THINGS THAT WERE GOOD TODAY:

1. _____

2. _____

3. _____

THE BEST THING IN MY DAY TODAY:

_____

_____

SOMETHING DIFFICULT I WAS ABLE TO WORK THROUGH:

_____

_____

DAILY DOODLE:

DATE: _____

THREE (LITTLE OR BIG) THINGS THAT WERE GOOD TODAY:

1. _____

2. _____

3. _____

THE BEST THING IN MY DAY TODAY:

_____

_____

SOMETHING DIFFICULT I WAS ABLE TO WORK THROUGH:

_____

_____

DAILY DOODLE:

DATE: _____

THREE (LITTLE OR BIG) THINGS THAT WERE GOOD TODAY:

1. _____

2. _____

3. _____

THE BEST THING IN MY DAY TODAY:

_____

_____

SOMETHING DIFFICULT I WAS ABLE TO WORK THROUGH:

_____

_____

DAILY DOODLE:

DATE: _____

THREE (LITTLE OR BIG) THINGS THAT WERE GOOD TODAY:

1. _____

2. _____

3. _____

THE BEST THING IN MY DAY TODAY:

_____

_____

SOMETHING DIFFICULT I WAS ABLE TO WORK THROUGH:

_____

_____

DAILY DOODLE:

DATE: _____

THREE (LITTLE OR BIG) THINGS THAT WERE GOOD TODAY:

1. _____

2. _____

3. _____

THE BEST THING IN MY DAY TODAY:

_____

_____

SOMETHING DIFFICULT I WAS ABLE TO WORK THROUGH:

_____

_____

DAILY DOODLE:

DATE:

THREE (LITTLE OR BIG) THINGS THAT WERE GOOD TODAY:

1.

2.

3.

THE BEST THING IN MY DAY TODAY:

SOMETHING DIFFICULT I WAS ABLE TO WORK THROUGH:

DAILY DOODLE:

DATE:

THREE (LITTLE OR BIG) THINGS THAT WERE GOOD TODAY:

1.

2.

3.

THE BEST THING IN MY DAY TODAY:

SOMETHING DIFFICULT I WAS ABLE TO WORK THROUGH:

DAILY DOODLE:

DATE: _____

THREE (LITTLE OR BIG) THINGS THAT WERE GOOD TODAY:

1. _____

2. _____

3. _____

THE BEST THING IN MY DAY TODAY:

_____

_____

SOMETHING DIFFICULT I WAS ABLE TO WORK THROUGH:

_____

_____

DAILY DOODLE:

DATE: _____

THREE (LITTLE OR BIG) THINGS THAT WERE GOOD TODAY:

1. _____

2. _____

3. _____

THE BEST THING IN MY DAY TODAY:

_____

_____

SOMETHING DIFFICULT I WAS ABLE TO WORK THROUGH:

_____

_____

DAILY DOODLE:

DATE: _____

THREE (LITTLE OR BIG) THINGS THAT WERE GOOD TODAY:

1. _____

2. _____

3. _____

THE BEST THING IN MY DAY TODAY:

_____

_____

SOMETHING DIFFICULT I WAS ABLE TO WORK THROUGH:

_____

_____

DAILY DOODLE:

DATE: _____

THREE (LITTLE OR BIG) THINGS THAT WERE GOOD TODAY:

1. _____

2. _____

3. _____

THE BEST THING IN MY DAY TODAY:

_____

_____

SOMETHING DIFFICULT I WAS ABLE TO WORK THROUGH:

_____

_____

DAILY DOODLE:

DATE: _____

THREE (LITTLE OR BIG) THINGS THAT WERE GOOD TODAY:

1. _____

2. _____

3. _____

THE BEST THING IN MY DAY TODAY:

_____

_____

SOMETHING DIFFICULT I WAS ABLE TO WORK THROUGH:

_____

_____

DAILY DOODLE:

DATE: _____

THREE (LITTLE OR BIG) THINGS THAT WERE GOOD TODAY:

1. _____

2. _____

3. _____

THE BEST THING IN MY DAY TODAY:

_____

_____

SOMETHING DIFFICULT I WAS ABLE TO WORK THROUGH:

_____

_____

DAILY DOODLE:

DATE: _____

THREE (LITTLE OR BIG) THINGS THAT WERE GOOD TODAY:

1. _____

2. _____

3. _____

THE BEST THING IN MY DAY TODAY:

_____

_____

SOMETHING DIFFICULT I WAS ABLE TO WORK THROUGH:

_____

_____

DAILY DOODLE:

DATE: _____

THREE (LITTLE OR BIG) THINGS THAT WERE GOOD TODAY:

1. _____

2. _____

3. _____

THE BEST THING IN MY DAY TODAY:

_____

_____

SOMETHING DIFFICULT I WAS ABLE TO WORK THROUGH:

_____

_____

DAILY DOODLE:

DATE: _____

THREE (LITTLE OR BIG) THINGS THAT WERE GOOD TODAY:

1. _____

2. _____

3. _____

THE BEST THING IN MY DAY TODAY:

_____

_____

SOMETHING DIFFICULT I WAS ABLE TO WORK THROUGH:

_____

_____

DAILY DOODLE:

DATE: _____

THREE (LITTLE OR BIG) THINGS THAT WERE GOOD TODAY:

1. _____

2. _____

3. _____

THE BEST THING IN MY DAY TODAY:

_____

_____

SOMETHING DIFFICULT I WAS ABLE TO WORK THROUGH:

_____

_____

DAILY DOODLE:

DATE:

THREE (LITTLE OR BIG) THINGS THAT WERE GOOD TODAY:

1.

2.

3.

THE BEST THING IN MY DAY TODAY:

SOMETHING DIFFICULT I WAS ABLE TO WORK THROUGH:

DAILY DOODLE:

DATE:

THREE (LITTLE OR BIG) THINGS THAT WERE GOOD TODAY:

1.

2.

3.

THE BEST THING IN MY DAY TODAY:

SOMETHING DIFFICULT I WAS ABLE TO WORK THROUGH:

DAILY DOODLE:

DATE: _____

THREE (LITTLE OR BIG) THINGS THAT WERE GOOD TODAY:

1. _____

2. _____

3. _____

THE BEST THING IN MY DAY TODAY:

_____

_____

SOMETHING DIFFICULT I WAS ABLE TO WORK THROUGH:

_____

_____

DAILY DOODLE:

DATE: _____

THREE (LITTLE OR BIG) THINGS THAT WERE GOOD TODAY:

1. _____

2. _____

3. _____

THE BEST THING IN MY DAY TODAY:

_____

_____

SOMETHING DIFFICULT I WAS ABLE TO WORK THROUGH:

_____

_____

DAILY DOODLE:

DATE: _____

THREE (LITTLE OR BIG) THINGS THAT WERE GOOD TODAY:

1. _____

2. _____

3. _____

THE BEST THING IN MY DAY TODAY:

_____

_____

SOMETHING DIFFICULT I WAS ABLE TO WORK THROUGH:

_____

_____

DAILY DOODLE:

DATE: _____

THREE (LITTLE OR BIG) THINGS THAT WERE GOOD TODAY:

1. _____

2. _____

3. _____

THE BEST THING IN MY DAY TODAY:

_____

_____

SOMETHING DIFFICULT I WAS ABLE TO WORK THROUGH:

_____

_____

DAILY DOODLE:

DATE: _____

THREE (LITTLE OR BIG) THINGS THAT WERE GOOD TODAY:

1. _____
2. _____
3. _____

THE BEST THING IN MY DAY TODAY:

_____
_____

SOMETHING DIFFICULT I WAS ABLE TO WORK THROUGH:

_____
_____

DAILY DOODLE:

DATE: _____

THREE (LITTLE OR BIG) THINGS THAT WERE GOOD TODAY:

1. _____
2. _____
3. _____

THE BEST THING IN MY DAY TODAY:

_____
_____

SOMETHING DIFFICULT I WAS ABLE TO WORK THROUGH:

_____
_____

DAILY DOODLE:

DATE: _____

THREE (LITTLE OR BIG) THINGS THAT WERE GOOD TODAY:

1. _____

2. _____

3. _____

THE BEST THING IN MY DAY TODAY:

_____

_____

SOMETHING DIFFICULT I WAS ABLE TO WORK THROUGH:

_____

_____

DAILY DOODLE:

DATE: _____

THREE (LITTLE OR BIG) THINGS THAT WERE GOOD TODAY:

1. _____

2. _____

3. _____

THE BEST THING IN MY DAY TODAY:

_____

_____

SOMETHING DIFFICULT I WAS ABLE TO WORK THROUGH:

_____

_____

DAILY DOODLE:

DATE: _____

THREE (LITTLE OR BIG) THINGS THAT WERE GOOD TODAY:

1. _____

2. _____

3. _____

THE BEST THING IN MY DAY TODAY:

_____

_____

SOMETHING DIFFICULT I WAS ABLE TO WORK THROUGH:

_____

_____

DAILY DOODLE:

DATE: _____

THREE (LITTLE OR BIG) THINGS THAT WERE GOOD TODAY:

1. _____

2. _____

3. _____

THE BEST THING IN MY DAY TODAY:

_____

_____

SOMETHING DIFFICULT I WAS ABLE TO WORK THROUGH:

_____

_____

DAILY DOODLE:

DATE: _____

THREE (LITTLE OR BIG) THINGS THAT WERE GOOD TODAY:

1. _____

2. _____

3. _____

THE BEST THING IN MY DAY TODAY:

_____

_____

SOMETHING DIFFICULT I WAS ABLE TO WORK THROUGH:

_____

_____

DAILY DOODLE:

DATE: _____

THREE (LITTLE OR BIG) THINGS THAT WERE GOOD TODAY:

1. _____

2. _____

3. _____

THE BEST THING IN MY DAY TODAY:

_____

_____

SOMETHING DIFFICULT I WAS ABLE TO WORK THROUGH:

_____

_____

DAILY DOODLE:

DATE: _____

THREE (LITTLE OR BIG) THINGS THAT WERE GOOD TODAY:

1. _____

2. _____

3. _____

THE BEST THING IN MY DAY TODAY:

_____

_____

SOMETHING DIFFICULT I WAS ABLE TO WORK THROUGH:

_____

_____

DAILY DOODLE:

DATE: _____

THREE (LITTLE OR BIG) THINGS THAT WERE GOOD TODAY:

1. _____

2. _____

3. _____

THE BEST THING IN MY DAY TODAY:

_____

_____

SOMETHING DIFFICULT I WAS ABLE TO WORK THROUGH:

_____

_____

DAILY DOODLE:

THREE (LITTLE OR BIG) THINGS THAT WERE GOOD TODAY:

1. _____

2. _____

3. _____

THE BEST THING IN MY DAY TODAY:

_____

_____

SOMETHING DIFFICULT I WAS ABLE TO WORK THROUGH:

_____

_____

DAILY DOODLE:

THREE (LITTLE OR BIG) THINGS THAT WERE GOOD TODAY:

1. _____

2. _____

3. _____

THE BEST THING IN MY DAY TODAY:

_____

_____

SOMETHING DIFFICULT I WAS ABLE TO WORK THROUGH:

_____

_____

DAILY DOODLE:

DATE: _____

THREE (LITTLE OR BIG) THINGS THAT WERE GOOD TODAY:

1. _____

2. _____

3. _____

THE BEST THING IN MY DAY TODAY:

_____

_____

SOMETHING DIFFICULT I WAS ABLE TO WORK THROUGH:

_____

_____

DAILY DOODLE:

DATE: _____

THREE (LITTLE OR BIG) THINGS THAT WERE GOOD TODAY:

1. _____

2. _____

3. _____

THE BEST THING IN MY DAY TODAY:

_____

_____

SOMETHING DIFFICULT I WAS ABLE TO WORK THROUGH:

_____

_____

DAILY DOODLE:

DATE: _____

THREE (LITTLE OR BIG) THINGS THAT WERE GOOD TODAY:

1. _____

2. _____

3. _____

THE BEST THING IN MY DAY TODAY:

_____

_____

SOMETHING DIFFICULT I WAS ABLE TO WORK THROUGH:

_____

_____

DAILY DOODLE:

DATE: _____

THREE (LITTLE OR BIG) THINGS THAT WERE GOOD TODAY:

1. _____

2. _____

3. _____

THE BEST THING IN MY DAY TODAY:

_____

_____

SOMETHING DIFFICULT I WAS ABLE TO WORK THROUGH:

_____

_____

DAILY DOODLE:

DATE: _____

THREE (LITTLE OR BIG) THINGS THAT WERE GOOD TODAY:

1. _____

2. _____

3. _____

THE BEST THING IN MY DAY TODAY:

_____

_____

SOMETHING DIFFICULT I WAS ABLE TO WORK THROUGH:

_____

_____

DAILY DOODLE:

DATE: _____

THREE (LITTLE OR BIG) THINGS THAT WERE GOOD TODAY:

1. _____

2. _____

3. _____

THE BEST THING IN MY DAY TODAY:

_____

_____

SOMETHING DIFFICULT I WAS ABLE TO WORK THROUGH:

_____

_____

DAILY DOODLE:

DATE: _____

THREE (LITTLE OR BIG) THINGS THAT WERE GOOD TODAY:

1. _____

2. _____

3. _____

THE BEST THING IN MY DAY TODAY:

_____

_____

SOMETHING DIFFICULT I WAS ABLE TO WORK THROUGH:

_____

_____

DAILY DOODLE:

DATE: _____

THREE (LITTLE OR BIG) THINGS THAT WERE GOOD TODAY:

1. _____

2. _____

3. _____

THE BEST THING IN MY DAY TODAY:

_____

_____

SOMETHING DIFFICULT I WAS ABLE TO WORK THROUGH:

_____

_____

DAILY DOODLE:

DATE: _____

THREE (LITTLE OR BIG) THINGS THAT WERE GOOD TODAY:

1. _____

2. _____

3. _____

THE BEST THING IN MY DAY TODAY:

_____

_____

SOMETHING DIFFICULT I WAS ABLE TO WORK THROUGH:

_____

_____

DAILY DOODLE:

DATE: _____

THREE (LITTLE OR BIG) THINGS THAT WERE GOOD TODAY:

1. _____

2. _____

3. _____

THE BEST THING IN MY DAY TODAY:

_____

_____

SOMETHING DIFFICULT I WAS ABLE TO WORK THROUGH:

_____

_____

DAILY DOODLE:

DATE: _____

THREE (LITTLE OR BIG) THINGS THAT WERE GOOD TODAY:

1. _____

2. _____

3. _____

THE BEST THING IN MY DAY TODAY:

_____

_____

SOMETHING DIFFICULT I WAS ABLE TO WORK THROUGH:

_____

_____

DAILY DOODLE:

DATE: _____

THREE (LITTLE OR BIG) THINGS THAT WERE GOOD TODAY:

1. _____

2. _____

3. _____

THE BEST THING IN MY DAY TODAY:

_____

_____

SOMETHING DIFFICULT I WAS ABLE TO WORK THROUGH:

_____

_____

DAILY DOODLE:

DATE: _____

THREE (LITTLE OR BIG) THINGS THAT WERE GOOD TODAY:

1. _____

2. _____

3. _____

THE BEST THING IN MY DAY TODAY:

_____

_____

SOMETHING DIFFICULT I WAS ABLE TO WORK THROUGH:

_____

_____

DAILY DOODLE:

DATE: _____

THREE (LITTLE OR BIG) THINGS THAT WERE GOOD TODAY:

1. _____

2. _____

3. _____

THE BEST THING IN MY DAY TODAY:

_____

_____

SOMETHING DIFFICULT I WAS ABLE TO WORK THROUGH:

_____

_____

DAILY DOODLE:

DATE: _____

THREE (LITTLE OR BIG) THINGS THAT WERE GOOD TODAY:

1. _____

2. _____

3. _____

THE BEST THING IN MY DAY TODAY:

_____

_____

SOMETHING DIFFICULT I WAS ABLE TO WORK THROUGH:

_____

_____

DAILY DOODLE:

DATE: _____

THREE (LITTLE OR BIG) THINGS THAT WERE GOOD TODAY:

1. _____

2. _____

3. _____

THE BEST THING IN MY DAY TODAY:

_____

_____

SOMETHING DIFFICULT I WAS ABLE TO WORK THROUGH:

_____

_____

DAILY DOODLE:

DATE: _____

THREE (LITTLE OR BIG) THINGS THAT WERE GOOD TODAY:

1. _____

2. _____

3. _____

THE BEST THING IN MY DAY TODAY:

_____

_____

SOMETHING DIFFICULT I WAS ABLE TO WORK THROUGH:

_____

_____

DAILY DOODLE:

DATE: _____

THREE (LITTLE OR BIG) THINGS THAT WERE GOOD TODAY:

1. _____

2. _____

3. _____

THE BEST THING IN MY DAY TODAY:

_____

_____

SOMETHING DIFFICULT I WAS ABLE TO WORK THROUGH:

_____

_____

DAILY DOODLE:

DATE: _____

THREE (LITTLE OR BIG) THINGS THAT WERE GOOD TODAY:

1. _____

2. _____

3. _____

THE BEST THING IN MY DAY TODAY:

_____

_____

SOMETHING DIFFICULT I WAS ABLE TO WORK THROUGH:

_____

_____

DAILY DOODLE:

DATE: _____

THREE (LITTLE OR BIG) THINGS THAT WERE GOOD TODAY:

1. _____

2. _____

3. _____

THE BEST THING IN MY DAY TODAY:

_____

_____

SOMETHING DIFFICULT I WAS ABLE TO WORK THROUGH:

_____

_____

DAILY DOODLE:

DATE: _____

THREE (LITTLE OR BIG) THINGS THAT WERE GOOD TODAY:

1. _____

2. _____

3. _____

THE BEST THING IN MY DAY TODAY:

_____

_____

SOMETHING DIFFICULT I WAS ABLE TO WORK THROUGH:

_____

_____

DAILY DOODLE:

DATE: _____

THREE (LITTLE OR BIG) THINGS THAT WERE GOOD TODAY:

1. _____

2. _____

3. _____

THE BEST THING IN MY DAY TODAY:

_____

_____

SOMETHING DIFFICULT I WAS ABLE TO WORK THROUGH:

_____

_____

DAILY DOODLE:

DATE: _____

THREE (LITTLE OR BIG) THINGS THAT WERE GOOD TODAY:

1. _____

2. _____

3. _____

THE BEST THING IN MY DAY TODAY:

_____

_____

SOMETHING DIFFICULT I WAS ABLE TO WORK THROUGH:

_____

_____

DAILY DOODLE:

DATE: _____

THREE (LITTLE OR BIG) THINGS THAT WERE GOOD TODAY:

1. _____

2. _____

3. _____

THE BEST THING IN MY DAY TODAY:

_____

_____

SOMETHING DIFFICULT I WAS ABLE TO WORK THROUGH:

_____

_____

DAILY DOODLE:

DATE: _____

THREE (LITTLE OR BIG) THINGS THAT WERE GOOD TODAY:
1. _____
2. _____
3. _____

THE BEST THING IN MY DAY TODAY:
_____
_____

SOMETHING DIFFICULT I WAS ABLE TO WORK THROUGH:
_____
_____

DAILY DOODLE:

DATE: _____

THREE (LITTLE OR BIG) THINGS THAT WERE GOOD TODAY:
1. _____
2. _____
3. _____

THE BEST THING IN MY DAY TODAY:
_____
_____

SOMETHING DIFFICULT I WAS ABLE TO WORK THROUGH:
_____
_____

DAILY DOODLE:

DATE: _____

THREE (LITTLE OR BIG) THINGS THAT WERE GOOD TODAY:

1. _____

2. _____

3. _____

THE BEST THING IN MY DAY TODAY:

_____

_____

SOMETHING DIFFICULT I WAS ABLE TO WORK THROUGH:

_____

_____

DAILY DOODLE:

DATE: _____

THREE (LITTLE OR BIG) THINGS THAT WERE GOOD TODAY:

1. _____

2. _____

3. _____

THE BEST THING IN MY DAY TODAY:

_____

_____

SOMETHING DIFFICULT I WAS ABLE TO WORK THROUGH:

_____

_____

DAILY DOODLE:

DATE: _____

THREE (LITTLE OR BIG) THINGS THAT WERE GOOD TODAY:

1. _____

2. _____

3. _____

THE BEST THING IN MY DAY TODAY:

_____

_____

SOMETHING DIFFICULT I WAS ABLE TO WORK THROUGH:

_____

_____

DAILY DOODLE:

DATE: _____

THREE (LITTLE OR BIG) THINGS THAT WERE GOOD TODAY:

1. _____

2. _____

3. _____

THE BEST THING IN MY DAY TODAY:

_____

_____

SOMETHING DIFFICULT I WAS ABLE TO WORK THROUGH:

_____

_____

DAILY DOODLE:

DATE: _____

THREE (LITTLE OR BIG) THINGS THAT WERE GOOD TODAY:

1. _____

2. _____

3. _____

THE BEST THING IN MY DAY TODAY:

_____

_____

SOMETHING DIFFICULT I WAS ABLE TO WORK THROUGH:

_____

_____

DAILY DOODLE:

DATE: _____

THREE (LITTLE OR BIG) THINGS THAT WERE GOOD TODAY:

1. _____

2. _____

3. _____

THE BEST THING IN MY DAY TODAY:

_____

_____

SOMETHING DIFFICULT I WAS ABLE TO WORK THROUGH:

_____

_____

DAILY DOODLE:

DATE: _____

THREE (LITTLE OR BIG) THINGS THAT WERE GOOD TODAY:

1. _____

2. _____

3. _____

THE BEST THING IN MY DAY TODAY:

_____

_____

SOMETHING DIFFICULT I WAS ABLE TO WORK THROUGH:

_____

_____

DAILY DOODLE:

DATE: _____

THREE (LITTLE OR BIG) THINGS THAT WERE GOOD TODAY:

1. _____

2. _____

3. _____

THE BEST THING IN MY DAY TODAY:

_____

_____

SOMETHING DIFFICULT I WAS ABLE TO WORK THROUGH:

_____

_____

DAILY DOODLE:

DATE: _____

THREE (LITTLE OR BIG) THINGS THAT WERE GOOD TODAY:

1. _____

2. _____

3. _____

THE BEST THING IN MY DAY TODAY:

_____

_____

SOMETHING DIFFICULT I WAS ABLE TO WORK THROUGH:

_____

_____

DAILY DOODLE:

DATE: _____

THREE (LITTLE OR BIG) THINGS THAT WERE GOOD TODAY:

1. _____

2. _____

3. _____

THE BEST THING IN MY DAY TODAY:

_____

_____

SOMETHING DIFFICULT I WAS ABLE TO WORK THROUGH:

_____

_____

DAILY DOODLE:

DATE: _____

THREE (LITTLE OR BIG) THINGS THAT WERE GOOD TODAY:

1. _____

2. _____

3. _____

THE BEST THING IN MY DAY TODAY:

_____

_____

SOMETHING DIFFICULT I WAS ABLE TO WORK THROUGH:

_____

_____

DAILY DOODLE:

DATE: _____

THREE (LITTLE OR BIG) THINGS THAT WERE GOOD TODAY:

1. _____

2. _____

3. _____

THE BEST THING IN MY DAY TODAY:

_____

_____

SOMETHING DIFFICULT I WAS ABLE TO WORK THROUGH:

_____

_____

DAILY DOODLE:

DATE: _____

THREE (LITTLE OR BIG) THINGS THAT WERE GOOD TODAY:

1. _____
2. _____
3. _____

THE BEST THING IN MY DAY TODAY:

_____
_____

SOMETHING DIFFICULT I WAS ABLE TO WORK THROUGH:

_____
_____

DAILY DOODLE:

DATE: _____

THREE (LITTLE OR BIG) THINGS THAT WERE GOOD TODAY:

1. _____
2. _____
3. _____

THE BEST THING IN MY DAY TODAY:

_____
_____

SOMETHING DIFFICULT I WAS ABLE TO WORK THROUGH:

_____
_____

DAILY DOODLE:

DATE: _____

THREE (LITTLE OR BIG) THINGS THAT WERE GOOD TODAY:

1. _____

2. _____

3. _____

THE BEST THING IN MY DAY TODAY:

_____

_____

SOMETHING DIFFICULT I WAS ABLE TO WORK THROUGH:

_____

_____

DAILY DOODLE:

DATE: _____

THREE (LITTLE OR BIG) THINGS THAT WERE GOOD TODAY:

1. _____

2. _____

3. _____

THE BEST THING IN MY DAY TODAY:

_____

_____

SOMETHING DIFFICULT I WAS ABLE TO WORK THROUGH:

_____

_____

DAILY DOODLE:

DATE: _____

THREE (LITTLE OR BIG) THINGS THAT WERE GOOD TODAY:

1. _____

2. _____

3. _____

THE BEST THING IN MY DAY TODAY:

_____

_____

SOMETHING DIFFICULT I WAS ABLE TO WORK THROUGH:

_____

_____

DAILY DOODLE:

DATE: _____

THREE (LITTLE OR BIG) THINGS THAT WERE GOOD TODAY:

1. _____

2. _____

3. _____

THE BEST THING IN MY DAY TODAY:

_____

_____

SOMETHING DIFFICULT I WAS ABLE TO WORK THROUGH:

_____

_____

DAILY DOODLE:

DATE: _____

THREE (LITTLE OR BIG) THINGS THAT WERE GOOD TODAY:

1. _____

2. _____

3. _____

THE BEST THING IN MY DAY TODAY:

_____

_____

SOMETHING DIFFICULT I WAS ABLE TO WORK THROUGH:

_____

_____

DAILY DOODLE:

DATE: _____

THREE (LITTLE OR BIG) THINGS THAT WERE GOOD TODAY:

1. _____

2. _____

3. _____

THE BEST THING IN MY DAY TODAY:

_____

_____

SOMETHING DIFFICULT I WAS ABLE TO WORK THROUGH:

_____

_____

DAILY DOODLE:

DATE: _____

THREE (LITTLE OR BIG) THINGS THAT WERE GOOD TODAY:

1. _____

2. _____

3. _____

THE BEST THING IN MY DAY TODAY:

_____

_____

SOMETHING DIFFICULT I WAS ABLE TO WORK THROUGH:

_____

_____

DAILY DOODLE:

DATE: _____

THREE (LITTLE OR BIG) THINGS THAT WERE GOOD TODAY:

1. _____

2. _____

3. _____

THE BEST THING IN MY DAY TODAY:

_____

_____

SOMETHING DIFFICULT I WAS ABLE TO WORK THROUGH:

_____

_____

DAILY DOODLE:

DATE: _____

THREE (LITTLE OR BIG) THINGS THAT WERE GOOD TODAY:

1. _____

2. _____

3. _____

THE BEST THING IN MY DAY TODAY:

_____

_____

SOMETHING DIFFICULT I WAS ABLE TO WORK THROUGH:

_____

_____

DAILY DOODLE:

DATE: _____

THREE (LITTLE OR BIG) THINGS THAT WERE GOOD TODAY:

1. _____

2. _____

3. _____

THE BEST THING IN MY DAY TODAY:

_____

_____

SOMETHING DIFFICULT I WAS ABLE TO WORK THROUGH:

_____

_____

DAILY DOODLE:

DATE: _____

THREE (LITTLE OR BIG) THINGS THAT WERE GOOD TODAY:

1. _____

2. _____

3. _____

THE BEST THING IN MY DAY TODAY:

_____

_____

SOMETHING DIFFICULT I WAS ABLE TO WORK THROUGH:

_____

_____

DAILY DOODLE:

DATE: _____

THREE (LITTLE OR BIG) THINGS THAT WERE GOOD TODAY:

1. _____

2. _____

3. _____

THE BEST THING IN MY DAY TODAY:

_____

_____

SOMETHING DIFFICULT I WAS ABLE TO WORK THROUGH:

_____

_____

DAILY DOODLE:

DATE: _____

THREE (LITTLE OR BIG) THINGS THAT WERE GOOD TODAY:

1. _____

2. _____

3. _____

THE BEST THING IN MY DAY TODAY:

_____

_____

SOMETHING DIFFICULT I WAS ABLE TO WORK THROUGH:

_____

_____

DAILY DOODLE:

DATE: _____

THREE (LITTLE OR BIG) THINGS THAT WERE GOOD TODAY:

1. _____

2. _____

3. _____

THE BEST THING IN MY DAY TODAY:

_____

_____

SOMETHING DIFFICULT I WAS ABLE TO WORK THROUGH:

_____

_____

DAILY DOODLE:

DATE: _____

THREE (LITTLE OR BIG) THINGS THAT WERE GOOD TODAY:

1. _____

2. _____

3. _____

THE BEST THING IN MY DAY TODAY:

_____

_____

SOMETHING DIFFICULT I WAS ABLE TO WORK THROUGH:

_____

_____

DAILY DOODLE:

DATE: _____

THREE (LITTLE OR BIG) THINGS THAT WERE GOOD TODAY:

1. _____

2. _____

3. _____

THE BEST THING IN MY DAY TODAY:

_____

_____

SOMETHING DIFFICULT I WAS ABLE TO WORK THROUGH:

_____

_____

DAILY DOODLE:

DATE: _____

THREE (LITTLE OR BIG) THINGS THAT WERE GOOD TODAY:

1. _____

2. _____

3. _____

THE BEST THING IN MY DAY TODAY:

_____

_____

SOMETHING DIFFICULT I WAS ABLE TO WORK THROUGH:

_____

_____

DAILY DOODLE:

DATE: _____

THREE (LITTLE OR BIG) THINGS THAT WERE GOOD TODAY:

1. _____

2. _____

3. _____

THE BEST THING IN MY DAY TODAY:

_____

_____

SOMETHING DIFFICULT I WAS ABLE TO WORK THROUGH:

_____

_____

DAILY DOODLE:

DATE: _____

THREE (LITTLE OR BIG) THINGS THAT WERE GOOD TODAY:

1. _____

2. _____

3. _____

THE BEST THING IN MY DAY TODAY:

_____

_____

SOMETHING DIFFICULT I WAS ABLE TO WORK THROUGH:

_____

_____

DAILY DOODLE:

DATE: _____

THREE (LITTLE OR BIG) THINGS THAT WERE GOOD TODAY:

1. _____

2. _____

3. _____

THE BEST THING IN MY DAY TODAY:

_____

_____

SOMETHING DIFFICULT I WAS ABLE TO WORK THROUGH:

_____

_____

DAILY DOODLE:

DATE: _____

THREE (LITTLE OR BIG) THINGS THAT WERE GOOD TODAY:

1. _____

2. _____

3. _____

THE BEST THING IN MY DAY TODAY:

_____

_____

SOMETHING DIFFICULT I WAS ABLE TO WORK THROUGH:

_____

_____

DAILY DOODLE:

DATE: _____

THREE (LITTLE OR BIG) THINGS THAT WERE GOOD TODAY:

1. _____

2. _____

3. _____

THE BEST THING IN MY DAY TODAY:

_____

_____

SOMETHING DIFFICULT I WAS ABLE TO WORK THROUGH:

_____

_____

DAILY DOODLE:

DATE: _____

THREE (LITTLE OR BIG) THINGS THAT WERE GOOD TODAY:

1. _____

2. _____

3. _____

THE BEST THING IN MY DAY TODAY:

_____

_____

SOMETHING DIFFICULT I WAS ABLE TO WORK THROUGH:

_____

_____

DAILY DOODLE:

DATE: _____

THREE (LITTLE OR BIG) THINGS THAT WERE GOOD TODAY:

1. _____

2. _____

3. _____

THE BEST THING IN MY DAY TODAY:

_____

_____

SOMETHING DIFFICULT I WAS ABLE TO WORK THROUGH:

_____

_____

DAILY DOODLE:

DATE: _____

THREE (LITTLE OR BIG) THINGS THAT WERE GOOD TODAY:

1. _____

2. _____

3. _____

THE BEST THING IN MY DAY TODAY:

_____

_____

SOMETHING DIFFICULT I WAS ABLE TO WORK THROUGH:

_____

_____

DAILY DOODLE:

DATE: _____

THREE (LITTLE OR BIG) THINGS THAT WERE GOOD TODAY:

1. _____

2. _____

3. _____

THE BEST THING IN MY DAY TODAY:

_____

_____

SOMETHING DIFFICULT I WAS ABLE TO WORK THROUGH:

_____

_____

DAILY DOODLE:

DATE:

THREE (LITTLE OR BIG) THINGS THAT WERE GOOD TODAY:

1.

2.

3.

THE BEST THING IN MY DAY TODAY:

SOMETHING DIFFICULT I WAS ABLE TO WORK THROUGH:

DAILY DOODLE:

DATE:

THREE (LITTLE OR BIG) THINGS THAT WERE GOOD TODAY:

1.

2.

3.

THE BEST THING IN MY DAY TODAY:

SOMETHING DIFFICULT I WAS ABLE TO WORK THROUGH:

DAILY DOODLE:

DATE: _____

THREE (LITTLE OR BIG) THINGS THAT WERE GOOD TODAY:

1. _____
2. _____
3. _____

THE BEST THING IN MY DAY TODAY:

_____
_____

SOMETHING DIFFICULT I WAS ABLE TO WORK THROUGH:

_____
_____

DAILY DOODLE:

DATE: _____

THREE (LITTLE OR BIG) THINGS THAT WERE GOOD TODAY:

1. _____
2. _____
3. _____

THE BEST THING IN MY DAY TODAY:

_____
_____

SOMETHING DIFFICULT I WAS ABLE TO WORK THROUGH:

_____
_____

DAILY DOODLE:

DATE: _____

THREE (LITTLE OR BIG) THINGS THAT WERE GOOD TODAY:

1. _____

2. _____

3. _____

THE BEST THING IN MY DAY TODAY:

_____

_____

SOMETHING DIFFICULT I WAS ABLE TO WORK THROUGH:

_____

_____

DAILY DOODLE:

DATE: _____

THREE (LITTLE OR BIG) THINGS THAT WERE GOOD TODAY:

1. _____

2. _____

3. _____

THE BEST THING IN MY DAY TODAY:

_____

_____

SOMETHING DIFFICULT I WAS ABLE TO WORK THROUGH:

_____

_____

DAILY DOODLE:

DATE: _____

THREE (LITTLE OR BIG) THINGS THAT WERE GOOD TODAY:

1. _____

2. _____

3. _____

THE BEST THING IN MY DAY TODAY:

_____

_____

SOMETHING DIFFICULT I WAS ABLE TO WORK THROUGH:

_____

_____

DAILY DOODLE:

DATE: _____

THREE (LITTLE OR BIG) THINGS THAT WERE GOOD TODAY:

1. _____

2. _____

3. _____

THE BEST THING IN MY DAY TODAY:

_____

_____

SOMETHING DIFFICULT I WAS ABLE TO WORK THROUGH:

_____

_____

DAILY DOODLE:

DATE: _____

THREE (LITTLE OR BIG) THINGS THAT WERE GOOD TODAY:

1. _____

2. _____

3. _____

THE BEST THING IN MY DAY TODAY:

_____

_____

SOMETHING DIFFICULT I WAS ABLE TO WORK THROUGH:

_____

_____

DAILY DOODLE:

DATE: _____

THREE (LITTLE OR BIG) THINGS THAT WERE GOOD TODAY:

1. _____

2. _____

3. _____

THE BEST THING IN MY DAY TODAY:

_____

_____

SOMETHING DIFFICULT I WAS ABLE TO WORK THROUGH:

_____

_____

DAILY DOODLE:

DATE: _____

THREE (LITTLE OR BIG) THINGS THAT WERE GOOD TODAY:

1. _____

2. _____

3. _____

THE BEST THING IN MY DAY TODAY:

_____

_____

SOMETHING DIFFICULT I WAS ABLE TO WORK THROUGH:

_____

_____

DAILY DOODLE:

DATE: _____

THREE (LITTLE OR BIG) THINGS THAT WERE GOOD TODAY:

1. _____

2. _____

3. _____

THE BEST THING IN MY DAY TODAY:

_____

_____

SOMETHING DIFFICULT I WAS ABLE TO WORK THROUGH:

_____

_____

DAILY DOODLE:

DATE: _____

THREE (LITTLE OR BIG) THINGS THAT WERE GOOD TODAY:

1. _____

2. _____

3. _____

THE BEST THING IN MY DAY TODAY:

_____

_____

SOMETHING DIFFICULT I WAS ABLE TO WORK THROUGH:

_____

_____

DAILY DOODLE:

DATE: _____

THREE (LITTLE OR BIG) THINGS THAT WERE GOOD TODAY:

1. _____

2. _____

3. _____

THE BEST THING IN MY DAY TODAY:

_____

_____

SOMETHING DIFFICULT I WAS ABLE TO WORK THROUGH:

_____

_____

DAILY DOODLE:

DATE: _____

THREE (LITTLE OR BIG) THINGS THAT WERE GOOD TODAY:

1. _____

2. _____

3. _____

THE BEST THING IN MY DAY TODAY:

_____

_____

SOMETHING DIFFICULT I WAS ABLE TO WORK THROUGH:

_____

_____

DAILY DOODLE:

DATE: _____

THREE (LITTLE OR BIG) THINGS THAT WERE GOOD TODAY:

1. _____

2. _____

3. _____

THE BEST THING IN MY DAY TODAY:

_____

_____

SOMETHING DIFFICULT I WAS ABLE TO WORK THROUGH:

_____

_____

DAILY DOODLE:

DATE: _____

THREE (LITTLE OR BIG) THINGS THAT WERE GOOD TODAY:

1. _____

2. _____

3. _____

THE BEST THING IN MY DAY TODAY:

_____

_____

SOMETHING DIFFICULT I WAS ABLE TO WORK THROUGH:

_____

_____

DAILY DOODLE:

DATE: _____

THREE (LITTLE OR BIG) THINGS THAT WERE GOOD TODAY:

1. _____

2. _____

3. _____

THE BEST THING IN MY DAY TODAY:

_____

_____

SOMETHING DIFFICULT I WAS ABLE TO WORK THROUGH:

_____

_____

DAILY DOODLE:

DATE: _____

THREE (LITTLE OR BIG) THINGS THAT WERE GOOD TODAY:

1. _____

2. _____

3. _____

THE BEST THING IN MY DAY TODAY:

_____

_____

SOMETHING DIFFICULT I WAS ABLE TO WORK THROUGH:

_____

_____

DAILY DOODLE:

DATE: _____

THREE (LITTLE OR BIG) THINGS THAT WERE GOOD TODAY:

1. _____

2. _____

3. _____

THE BEST THING IN MY DAY TODAY:

_____

_____

SOMETHING DIFFICULT I WAS ABLE TO WORK THROUGH:

_____

_____

DAILY DOODLE:

DATE: _____

THREE (LITTLE OR BIG) THINGS THAT WERE GOOD TODAY:

1. _____

2. _____

3. _____

THE BEST THING IN MY DAY TODAY:

_____

_____

SOMETHING DIFFICULT I WAS ABLE TO WORK THROUGH:

_____

_____

DAILY DOODLE:

DATE: _____

THREE (LITTLE OR BIG) THINGS THAT WERE GOOD TODAY:

1. _____

2. _____

3. _____

THE BEST THING IN MY DAY TODAY:

_____

_____

SOMETHING DIFFICULT I WAS ABLE TO WORK THROUGH:

_____

_____

DAILY DOODLE:

DATE: _____

THREE (LITTLE OR BIG) THINGS THAT WERE GOOD TODAY:

1. _____

2. _____

3. _____

THE BEST THING IN MY DAY TODAY:

_____

_____

SOMETHING DIFFICULT I WAS ABLE TO WORK THROUGH:

_____

_____

DAILY DOODLE:

DATE: _____

THREE (LITTLE OR BIG) THINGS THAT WERE GOOD TODAY:

1. _____

2. _____

3. _____

THE BEST THING IN MY DAY TODAY:

_____

_____

SOMETHING DIFFICULT I WAS ABLE TO WORK THROUGH:

_____

_____

DAILY DOODLE:

DATE: _____

THREE (LITTLE OR BIG) THINGS THAT WERE GOOD TODAY:

1. _____
2. _____
3. _____

THE BEST THING IN MY DAY TODAY:

_____

_____

SOMETHING DIFFICULT I WAS ABLE TO WORK THROUGH:

_____

_____

DAILY DOODLE:

DATE: _____

THREE (LITTLE OR BIG) THINGS THAT WERE GOOD TODAY:

1. _____
2. _____
3. _____

THE BEST THING IN MY DAY TODAY:

_____

_____

SOMETHING DIFFICULT I WAS ABLE TO WORK THROUGH:

_____

_____

DAILY DOODLE:

DATE: _____

THREE (LITTLE OR BIG) THINGS THAT WERE GOOD TODAY:

1. _____

2. _____

3. _____

THE BEST THING IN MY DAY TODAY:

_____

_____

SOMETHING DIFFICULT I WAS ABLE TO WORK THROUGH:

_____

_____

DAILY DOODLE:

DATE: _____

THREE (LITTLE OR BIG) THINGS THAT WERE GOOD TODAY:

1. _____

2. _____

3. _____

THE BEST THING IN MY DAY TODAY:

_____

_____

SOMETHING DIFFICULT I WAS ABLE TO WORK THROUGH:

_____

_____

DAILY DOODLE:

DATE: _____

THREE (LITTLE OR BIG) THINGS THAT WERE GOOD TODAY:

1. _____

2. _____

3. _____

THE BEST THING IN MY DAY TODAY:

_____

_____

SOMETHING DIFFICULT I WAS ABLE TO WORK THROUGH:

_____

_____

DAILY DOODLE:

DATE: _____

THREE (LITTLE OR BIG) THINGS THAT WERE GOOD TODAY:

1. _____

2. _____

3. _____

THE BEST THING IN MY DAY TODAY:

_____

_____

SOMETHING DIFFICULT I WAS ABLE TO WORK THROUGH:

_____

_____

DAILY DOODLE:

DATE: _____

THREE (LITTLE OR BIG) THINGS THAT WERE GOOD TODAY:

1. _____

2. _____

3. _____

THE BEST THING IN MY DAY TODAY:

_____

_____

SOMETHING DIFFICULT I WAS ABLE TO WORK THROUGH:

_____

_____

DAILY DOODLE:

DATE: _____

THREE (LITTLE OR BIG) THINGS THAT WERE GOOD TODAY:

1. _____

2. _____

3. _____

THE BEST THING IN MY DAY TODAY:

_____

_____

SOMETHING DIFFICULT I WAS ABLE TO WORK THROUGH:

_____

_____

DAILY DOODLE:

DATE: _____

THREE (LITTLE OR BIG) THINGS THAT WERE GOOD TODAY:

1. _____

2. _____

3. _____

THE BEST THING IN MY DAY TODAY:

_____

_____

SOMETHING DIFFICULT I WAS ABLE TO WORK THROUGH:

_____

_____

DAILY DOODLE:

DATE: _____

THREE (LITTLE OR BIG) THINGS THAT WERE GOOD TODAY:

1. _____

2. _____

3. _____

THE BEST THING IN MY DAY TODAY:

_____

_____

SOMETHING DIFFICULT I WAS ABLE TO WORK THROUGH:

_____

_____

DAILY DOODLE:

DATE: _____

THREE (LITTLE OR BIG) THINGS THAT WERE GOOD TODAY:

1. _____

2. _____

3. _____

THE BEST THING IN MY DAY TODAY:

_____

_____

SOMETHING DIFFICULT I WAS ABLE TO WORK THROUGH:

_____

_____

DAILY DOODLE:

DATE: _____

THREE (LITTLE OR BIG) THINGS THAT WERE GOOD TODAY:

1. _____

2. _____

3. _____

THE BEST THING IN MY DAY TODAY:

_____

_____

SOMETHING DIFFICULT I WAS ABLE TO WORK THROUGH:

_____

_____

DAILY DOODLE:

DATE: _____

THREE (LITTLE OR BIG) THINGS THAT WERE GOOD TODAY:

1. _____

2. _____

3. _____

THE BEST THING IN MY DAY TODAY:

_____

_____

SOMETHING DIFFICULT I WAS ABLE TO WORK THROUGH:

_____

_____

DAILY DOODLE:

DATE: _____

THREE (LITTLE OR BIG) THINGS THAT WERE GOOD TODAY:

1. _____

2. _____

3. _____

THE BEST THING IN MY DAY TODAY:

_____

_____

SOMETHING DIFFICULT I WAS ABLE TO WORK THROUGH:

_____

_____

DAILY DOODLE:

DATE: _____

THREE (LITTLE OR BIG) THINGS THAT WERE GOOD TODAY:

1. _____

2. _____

3. _____

THE BEST THING IN MY DAY TODAY:

_____

_____

SOMETHING DIFFICULT I WAS ABLE TO WORK THROUGH:

_____

_____

DAILY DOODLE:

DATE: _____

THREE (LITTLE OR BIG) THINGS THAT WERE GOOD TODAY:

1. _____

2. _____

3. _____

THE BEST THING IN MY DAY TODAY:

_____

_____

SOMETHING DIFFICULT I WAS ABLE TO WORK THROUGH:

_____

_____

DAILY DOODLE:

DATE: _____

THREE (LITTLE OR BIG) THINGS THAT WERE GOOD TODAY:

1. _____

2. _____

3. _____

THE BEST THING IN MY DAY TODAY:

_____

_____

SOMETHING DIFFICULT I WAS ABLE TO WORK THROUGH:

_____

_____

DAILY DOODLE:

DATE: _____

THREE (LITTLE OR BIG) THINGS THAT WERE GOOD TODAY:

1. _____

2. _____

3. _____

THE BEST THING IN MY DAY TODAY:

_____

_____

SOMETHING DIFFICULT I WAS ABLE TO WORK THROUGH:

_____

_____

DAILY DOODLE:

DATE: _____

THREE (LITTLE OR BIG) THINGS THAT WERE GOOD TODAY:

1. _____

2. _____

3. _____

THE BEST THING IN MY DAY TODAY:

_____

_____

SOMETHING DIFFICULT I WAS ABLE TO WORK THROUGH:

_____

_____

DAILY DOODLE:

DATE: _____

THREE (LITTLE OR BIG) THINGS THAT WERE GOOD TODAY:

1. _____

2. _____

3. _____

THE BEST THING IN MY DAY TODAY:

_____

_____

SOMETHING DIFFICULT I WAS ABLE TO WORK THROUGH:

_____

_____

DAILY DOODLE:

DATE: _____

THREE (LITTLE OR BIG) THINGS THAT WERE GOOD TODAY:

1. _____

2. _____

3. _____

THE BEST THING IN MY DAY TODAY:

_____

_____

SOMETHING DIFFICULT I WAS ABLE TO WORK THROUGH:

_____

_____

DAILY DOODLE:

DATE: _____

THREE (LITTLE OR BIG) THINGS THAT WERE GOOD TODAY:

1. _____

2. _____

3. _____

THE BEST THING IN MY DAY TODAY:

_____

_____

SOMETHING DIFFICULT I WAS ABLE TO WORK THROUGH:

_____

_____

DAILY DOODLE:

DATE: _____

THREE (LITTLE OR BIG) THINGS THAT WERE GOOD TODAY:

1. _____

2. _____

3. _____

THE BEST THING IN MY DAY TODAY:

_____

_____

SOMETHING DIFFICULT I WAS ABLE TO WORK THROUGH:

_____

_____

DAILY DOODLE:

DATE: _____

THREE (LITTLE OR BIG) THINGS THAT WERE GOOD TODAY:

1. _____

2. _____

3. _____

THE BEST THING IN MY DAY TODAY:

_____

_____

SOMETHING DIFFICULT I WAS ABLE TO WORK THROUGH:

_____

_____

DAILY DOODLE:

DATE: _____

THREE (LITTLE OR BIG) THINGS THAT WERE GOOD TODAY:

1. _____

2. _____

3. _____

THE BEST THING IN MY DAY TODAY:

_____

_____

SOMETHING DIFFICULT I WAS ABLE TO WORK THROUGH:

_____

_____

DAILY DOODLE:

DATE: _____

THREE (LITTLE OR BIG) THINGS THAT WERE GOOD TODAY:

1. _____

2. _____

3. _____

THE BEST THING IN MY DAY TODAY:

_____

_____

SOMETHING DIFFICULT I WAS ABLE TO WORK THROUGH:

_____

_____

DAILY DOODLE:

DATE: _____

THREE (LITTLE OR BIG) THINGS THAT WERE GOOD TODAY:

1. _____

2. _____

3. _____

THE BEST THING IN MY DAY TODAY:

_____

_____

SOMETHING DIFFICULT I WAS ABLE TO WORK THROUGH:

_____

_____

DAILY DOODLE:

DATE: _____

THREE (LITTLE OR BIG) THINGS THAT WERE GOOD TODAY:

1. _____

2. _____

3. _____

THE BEST THING IN MY DAY TODAY:

_____

_____

SOMETHING DIFFICULT I WAS ABLE TO WORK THROUGH:

_____

_____

DAILY DOODLE:

DATE: _____

THREE (LITTLE OR BIG) THINGS THAT WERE GOOD TODAY:

1. _____

2. _____

3. _____

THE BEST THING IN MY DAY TODAY:

_____

_____

SOMETHING DIFFICULT I WAS ABLE TO WORK THROUGH:

_____

_____

DAILY DOODLE:

DATE: _____

THREE (LITTLE OR BIG) THINGS THAT WERE GOOD TODAY:

1. _____

2. _____

3. _____

THE BEST THING IN MY DAY TODAY:

_____

_____

SOMETHING DIFFICULT I WAS ABLE TO WORK THROUGH:

_____

_____

DAILY DOODLE:

DATE: _____

THREE (LITTLE OR BIG) THINGS THAT WERE GOOD TODAY:

1. _____

2. _____

3. _____

THE BEST THING IN MY DAY TODAY:

_____

_____

SOMETHING DIFFICULT I WAS ABLE TO WORK THROUGH:

_____

_____

DAILY DOODLE:

DATE: _____

THREE (LITTLE OR BIG) THINGS THAT WERE GOOD TODAY:

1. _____

2. _____

3. _____

THE BEST THING IN MY DAY TODAY:

_____

_____

SOMETHING DIFFICULT I WAS ABLE TO WORK THROUGH:

_____

_____

DAILY DOODLE:

DATE: _____

THREE (LITTLE OR BIG) THINGS THAT WERE GOOD TODAY:

1. _____

2. _____

3. _____

THE BEST THING IN MY DAY TODAY:

_____

_____

SOMETHING DIFFICULT I WAS ABLE TO WORK THROUGH:

_____

_____

_____

DAILY DOODLE:

DATE: _____

THREE (LITTLE OR BIG) THINGS THAT WERE GOOD TODAY:

1. _____

2. _____

3. _____

THE BEST THING IN MY DAY TODAY:

_____

_____

SOMETHING DIFFICULT I WAS ABLE TO WORK THROUGH:

_____

_____

_____

DAILY DOODLE:

DATE: _____

THREE (LITTLE OR BIG) THINGS THAT WERE GOOD TODAY:

1. _____

2. _____

3. _____

THE BEST THING IN MY DAY TODAY:

_____

_____

SOMETHING DIFFICULT I WAS ABLE TO WORK THROUGH:

_____

_____

DAILY DOODLE:

DATE: _____

THREE (LITTLE OR BIG) THINGS THAT WERE GOOD TODAY:

1. _____

2. _____

3. _____

THE BEST THING IN MY DAY TODAY:

_____

_____

SOMETHING DIFFICULT I WAS ABLE TO WORK THROUGH:

_____

_____

DAILY DOODLE:

Made in the USA
Lexington, KY
08 December 2019

58301119R00068